it is well

WALKING AWAY FROM ANXIETY
AND INTO GOD'S WORD

by
SARAH MORRISON

study suggestions

Thank you for choosing this study to help you dig into God's Word. We are so passionate about women getting into Scripture, and we are praying that this study will be a tool to help you do that. Here are a few tips to help you get the most from this study:

• Before you begin, take time to look into the context of the book. Find out who wrote it and learn about the cultural climate it was written in, as well as where it fits on the biblical timeline. Then take time to read through the entire book of the Bible we are studying if you are able. This will help you to get the big picture of the book and will aid in comprehension, interpretation, and application.

• Start your study time with prayer. Ask God to help you understand what you are reading and allow it to transform you (Psalm 119:18).

• Look into the context of the book as well as the specific passage.

• Before reading what is written in the study, read the assigned passage! Repetitive reading is one of the best ways to study God's Word. Read it several times, if you are able, before going on to the study. Read in several translations if you find it helpful.

• As you read the text, mark down observations and questions. Write down things that stand out to you, things that you notice, or things that you don't understand. Look up important words in a dictionary or interlinear Bible.

• Look for things like verbs, commands, and references to God. Notice key terms and themes throughout the passage.

• After you have worked through the text, read what is written in the study. Take time to look up any cross-references mentioned as you study.

• Then work through the questions provided in the book. Read and answer them prayerfully.

• Paraphrase or summarize the passage, or even just one verse from the passage. Putting it into your own words helps you to slow down and think through every word.

• Focus your heart on the character of God that you have seen in this passage. What do you learn about God from the passage you have studied? Adore Him and praise Him for who He is.

• Think and pray through application and how this passage should change you. Get specific with yourself. Resist the urge to apply the passage to others. Do you have sin to confess? How should this passage impact your attitude toward people or circumstances? Does the passage command you to do something? Do you need to trust Him for something in your life? How does the truth of the gospel impact your everyday life?

We recommend you have a Bible, pen, highlighters, and journal as you work through this study. We recommend that ball point pens instead of gel pens be used in the study book to prevent smearing. Here are several other optional resources that you may find helpful as you study:

• www.blueletterbible.org This free website is a great resource for digging deeper. You can find translation comparison, an interlinear option to look at words in the original languages, Bible dictionaries, and even commentary.

• A Dictionary. If looking up words in the Hebrew and Greek feels intimidating, look up words in English. Often times we assume we know the meaning of a word, but looking it up and seeing its definition can help us understand a passage better.

• A double-spaced copy of the text. You can use a website like www.biblegateway.com to copy the text of a passage and print out a double-spaced copy to be able to mark on easily. Circle, underline, highlight, draw arrows, and mark in any way you would like to help you dig deeper and work through a passage.

week one

DAY ONE

Introduction

For God has not given us a spirit of fear, but one of power, love, and sound judgment.

2 Timothy 1:7

Paul's second letter to Timothy comes at a tumultuous time for both himself and for Timothy. Paul is nearing the end of his life. He is expecting to die soon by execution from the Roman government. The apostle is burdened, knowing that the gospel must continue to go out. There has to be someone to whom he can pass the proverbial torch of church planting and evangelism to. This is where Timothy comes in.

Timothy was Paul's protégé. Paul refers to him as a son multiple times, and in his two letters to Timothy he seeks to give him godly wisdom about how to be a pastor and church planter—doing so with excellence despite his young age. Can you imagine the pressure that this letter conveys pressing in on all sides? Paul knows death is around the corner; he can practically see the whites of death's eyes before him. Timothy is about to lose his mentor and is being thrust into a position of authority in the church. But this pressure to fold into fear, Paul conveys, is not from God. In 2 Timothy 1:7 Paul makes a bold assertion: a spirit of fear is not from the Lord, but power, love, and sound judgement are.

As believers in Jesus Christ, we're also recipients of the Holy Spirit. He's our Guide, our Counselor, our Intercessor—He makes holiness possible for us. Through Him we are given a spirit of power, love, and sound judgement. We have these traits available to us through His working within us. We can rest assured in this promise. He is continually and constantly offering us His power, strength, wisdom, and love. He is perpetually offering us access to His fruit.

Do you see how powerful that is? The God, the only true God, the Founder of the universe, the Knower of all things, the definition of goodness and perfection, lives within us. He spoke the universe into existence, and we have access to His power and His goodness through the indwelling Holy Spirit. The Holy Spirit is our seal for the eternal inheritance we have through Christ. He is our provision of good, godly fruit in our lives. He is the fount from which we are afforded the ability to flee from sin and death.

From this we can also know that anything that is not powerful, loving, or discerning is from our flesh or the enemy, not the Holy Spirit within us. Anxiety, doubt, depression, fear, weakness—these things are not from God. God certainly uses these things in our lives (Romans 8:28). He absolutely draws us closer to Him through these tendencies, but they themselves are not from the Father. They are from the fall. If something doesn't look like the Father, Son, or Holy Spirit, then it is not from God. Our struggles with worry and doubt are no exception. These things aren't sent to us from God. He simply uses them, redeems us from them, and receives glory from them all the while.

This walk through the Bible with anxiety in mind is not meant to be a treatment for profound mental illnesses, though I pray it will be helpful for those in every situation. This study is not meant to replace any counsel you have received from licensed professionals and pastors that know you and have walked with you through your experiences. What this study is intended for is helping you in knowing God, loving Him better, and hopefully, giving tools that enable, encourage, and empower you in your journey to flee from anxious thoughts and run to the Father's arms. By the power of the Holy Spirit, let's become victorious over the fears that seek to destroy us. Together, let's build up the qualities of power, love, and discernment in our lives.

By the power of the Holy Spirit, let's become victorious over the fears that seek to destroy us.

1. How can you discern whether or not something is from God?

_____

2. Compare and contrast fear and anxiety with love, power, and sound judgment—how can recognizing these things help you to fight against anxiety and fear?

_____

3. The Holy Spirit empowers believers to flee from fearful and anxious thoughts. How does such knowledge encourage your own thoughts?

_____

week one

DAY TWO

The Prescription

*Don't worry about anything, but in everything, through prayer and
petition with thanksgiving, present your requests to God.*

Philippians 4:6

When anxious thoughts pervade our hearts and minds, the last thing we want to hear from our spouse, friends, or family is not to worry about it! Those words seem to exasperate the situation, overwhelming us more. It's a frustrating sentiment. If anxiety were more like a switch that you could flip at anytime, wouldn't you choose to flip it? Don't they understand that? It is easy for us to distance ourselves from our loved ones who give this advice with good intentions. It can make us feel misunderstood. It can make us feel illegitimate. It can belittle us.

This isn't what Paul the apostle is doing in this short verse from Philippians though. He isn't saying, "Don't worry. There's nothing to worry about. Why are you like this?" Instead, he's acknowledging a problem that is an epidemic in the human experience, and he is providing a practical prescription to take when fear and worries overtake us. Paul's advice doesn't stop at "just don't worry." He carries on giving practical application in our lives. He doesn't merely say, "worrying is sinful, you must stop at once." He gives the worriers, the doubters, and the fearful hope for reprieve. He gives us a prescription to fill.

Paul tells us not to worry and then carries on. He tells us in everything we can request our wants and needs to God through prayer and petition. *In everything.* There is no boundary or limit to what we can go to God for. Whether we are worried about losing our job, or worried about death and illness, or worried about what to make for dinner—even if we can't verbally express the reason for our worry, even if we don't know what we're worried about—all of it, every single thing, we can take before the throne of God, and He will lend us His divine ear.

Through prayer and petition we make our requests known to God. Not only does that mean that we *can* talk to Him, it means that we *must* talk to Him. Our prayer, or lack thereof, can help or hinder our triumph in fleeing from sin and into the arms of God. Prayer can be difficult. It can be hard to know what to say to someone who already knows it all, but we pray not for God's benefit, but our own. God knows when anxiety plagues us, He knows our sinful tendencies, He knows what causes us to doubt. He knows it all. But prayer helps us to cultivate a deeper walk with the Almighty. By it we give Him our worries and doubts, submitting them to Him for His action, not our own action. Through prayer we yield ourselves to God's work within us. When we pray, our souls are changed. We know God better through prayer. He works in us through prayer. He refines us through prayer like metals in a flame, striking out the impurities that keep us from being holy as He is holy.

Most of us aren't people who can simply turn off the bulb of anxiety in our brains, but that doesn't mean that we are a people without any hope of freedom from anxiety. It does mean that we make active choices toward obedience though. It means that we submit ourselves to the fires of refinement, knowing that though it will be painful and challenging, it will be worth it for the sake of sanctification and holiness. Let's submit to making our worries, requests, and fears known to God, faithfully and relentlessly petitioning to our Father who can change us and our circumstances.

Through prayer we yield ourselves to God's work within us.

1. Spend some time thinking about the purpose of prayer. Why is it important to pray? How does it change us?

2. What reasons are there to trust God with our petitions and requests?

3. Spend some time in prayer, bringing your petitions and requests before the Father, asking that He would help you to be free from worry and doubt.

week one

—

DAY THREE

1 Samuel 1:12-20

While she continued praying in the Lord's presence, Eli watched her mouth. Hannah was praying silently, and though her lips were moving, her voice could not be heard. Eli thought she was drunk and said to her, "How long are you going to be drunk? Get rid of your wine!" "No, my lord," Hannah replied. "I am a woman with a broken heart. I haven't had any wine or beer; I've been pouring out my heart before the Lord. Don't think of me as a wicked woman; I've been praying from the depth of my anguish and resentment." Eli responded, "Go in peace, and may the God of Israel grant the request you've made of him." "May your servant find favor with you," she replied. Then Hannah went on her way; she ate and no longer looked despondent. The next morning Elkanah and Hannah got up early to worship before the Lord. Afterward, they returned home to Ramah. Then Elkanah was intimate with his wife Hannah, and the Lord remembered her. After some time, Hannah conceived and gave birth to a son. She named him Samuel, because she said, "I requested him from the Lord."

Hannah was a woman of God, seeking after her Lord in prayer. She was afflicted. Being unable to bear children caused her to be mocked by others in her presence. She felt the cultural sting of a closed womb. She felt alone in her affliction. However, she didn't run away from God in her frustration; she ran *to* Him instead. Eli the priest thought she was drunk while she was praying, but she wasn't. Hannah was simply vulnerable before God. She was pleading before the throne of the Father, asking that He would mend her broken heart, asking that He would intervene. *I've been praying from the depth of my anguish and resentment.* Hannah prayed with everything she had inside of her; she allowed the depth of anguish and resentment within her soul to overflow into a petition to the Father.

When Hannah experienced desperation, she fled to the Lord in prayer. When Hannah needed consolation, she sought it in God. When Hannah needed intervention, she knew she must bow before the throne of grace and plead her case before the Father. Hannah approached God in her great distress, and He heard her. In fact, verse 19 tells us that the Lord *remembered* her. He did not merely hear her. He did not simply listen to her groaning, humoring her for the sake of pity. He remembered her, and He chose to grant Hannah's request. She conceived a son and dedicated him to the Lord.

Eli, the priest, thought that Hannah had been drunk when she prayed. She wasn't calmly kneeling, hands folded, and mouth shut. She was praying earnestly, her lips moving but not forming words. She poured herself out before the Lord in her grief and distress. Hannah gives us an example to follow when we pray; she shows us a posture of earnestness and sincerity. She prays in a way slightly reminiscent of Luke 18:9-14, crying out to God in a desperate spirit instead of demure appearance. It's okay to lay yourself bare before God in vulnerability.

Hannah prayed knowing that her groans were not falling on deaf ears. God hears us. Psalm 34:15 testifies to that fact. He hears His children, the ones made righteous by faith in Jesus Christ. His ears are open to us when we cry out to Him. We pray because of God's mercy, not because we deserve our requests (Daniel 9:18). We pray knowing of God's righteousness, abundant compassion, and worthiness to be praised, not because of our worthiness of reward. Prayer changes *us*, not God. Prayer molds our heart toward godly affection.

John Piper famously said, "Prayer causes things to happen that wouldn't happen if you didn't pray." Prayer doesn't change God's plan, but it does change our hearts. It changes our desires. Unceasing, faithful, and faith-filled prayer to an unchanging, gracious Savior can break the chains that bind us to anxiety. Prayer can treat the source and the symptoms of anxiety. It changes the very foundation of who we are by aligning us with God Himself. When we pray like Hannah, with earnestness and transparency, we can rest in the knowledge that God will remember us. He hears the cries of His children. He hears us from the bottom of our broken heart and rescues us from the depths of anxiety. He contends for us. He remembers His people.

He hears the cries of His children.

1. Why is it important to pray when we become consumed with anxiety?

_____

2. How can Hannah's testimony bolster your confidence in praying to the Lord?

_____

3. What do you find most difficult in your personal prayer life? Spend some time before the Lord, giving Him this burden and asking that He would grow you in this area.

_____

week one

—

DAY FOUR

Romans 8:26-27

In the same way the Spirit also helps us in our weakness because we do not know what to pray for as we should, but the Spirit himself intercedes for us with unspoken groanings. And he who searches our hearts knows the mind of the Spirit, because he intercedes for the saints according to the will of God.

Philippians told us about the importance of praying—having a conversation with God about the things that make us anxious and requesting that He free and heal us. Hannah's story is a testimony to the faithfulness of God to hear our prayers. But what about those times where it feels like we can't even speak, can't even move our lips? It is not uncommon that in our weakness we don't know how to pray. We find ourselves at a loss for words, weeping and gritting our teeth. But the Holy Spirit doesn't leave us to ourselves in that place. Even in the thick of darkness the Lord will provide for us. He will hear us.

Paul is telling the church of Rome in Romans 8:26-27 that the Holy Spirit takes up words on our behalf. He intercedes for us. He prays for us when we don't have the words to bring before the Father. He attentively and tenderly takes the requests and petitions from the deepest well of our soul and He carries them up, placing them before God the Father, pleading our case for us. When we don't know what to pray, He finds the words. When we don't know how to pray, He does it for us. When we're trudging through the mire and muck, the Spirit picks us up and upholds us through prayer.

It seems sort of surreal that this could take place—that one member of the Godhead could pray on our behalf to another member of the Trinity. Perfect oneness and unity on display alongside perfect distinction. He has made a way, no matter what, for us to pray to Him and make known to Him the struggles that bear down on our back. That's how profoundly the Lord cares for us. That's how greatly He wants to bear our griefs for us. That's how much He wants us to feel freedom from anxiety. The Lord doesn't give us the remedy for our anxiety in Philippians 4:6 and then leave us unequipped. The prescription He provides is not unattainable. The Lord makes a way for us to pray, even when it feels like our lips cannot form the words.

The verse also draws to our minds that the Lord searches our hearts. He perceives our deepest pains and struggles because of how well He knows us. He knows our whole being—our physicality, our thoughts, and our preferences. We are completely transparent before Him, so there is no need to doubt that the Holy Spirit sympathizes with us when we experience anxious thoughts, suspicions, or depression. Not only does He sympathize with us, but He also invites us into healing through the prayers we cannot even pronounce. The Holy Spirit helps us when we can't seem to verbalize our requests to the Father.

Silent prayer is not purposeless. It's not a sin when you feel like you don't have the words to pray. Even still, don't forsake planting yourself before the Father's feet. Though our mouths may merely groan unable to form words or sentences, when we place ourselves before the throne of God in silence, we know that the Holy Spirit is devotedly communicating our requests for us. He is advocating on our behalf. In so doing, we defy the work of Satan and snuff-out the flaming darts of our enemy. Wordlessness in God's presence with reliance on the Holy Spirit to take up our cause, dependence on the sacrifice of Christ to make us whole, and yielding ourselves before the Father is purposeful, harmonious prayer to the Lord.

The Holy Spirit helps us when we can't seem to verbalize our requests to the Father.

1. What comfort can this afford you today?

_____

2. In what ways does this give you confidence that victory over anxiety is possible?

_____

3. Spend some time in silent prayer before the Lord, relying on the Holy Spirit to take up the words for you when worries and fears overwhelm you.

_____

week one

DAY FIVE

Matthew 11:28-30

Come to me, all of you who are weary and burdened, and I will give you rest.
Take up my yoke and learn from me, because I am lowly and humble in heart, and you
will find rest for your souls. For my yoke is easy and my burden is light.

Jesus addresses His words to those who are wearied and burdened. That means all of us, doesn't it? He invites those who are tired, frustrated, and bogged down by the throes of life into security with Him. When anxious thoughts invade our hearts and minds, we often feel alone. We feel tired, exhausted from the war that is waging within us, torn apart by the battle between lies and truth. This passage from Matthew 11 offers us hope through the presence of Jesus Christ in our lives though. These few brief verses remind us of where we can and should run in our exhaustion. This is another prescription from the mouth of God to aid us in remedying our heaviest thoughts.

Jesus invites us to Himself. He's the Giver of life, the Author of peace, our perfect God, and He invites us to come to Him with all that we carry. With our weariness, we're invited to sit at His feet. With our burdens, we're invited to recline at His side. Not only does Paul remind us that we can petition God in our anxiety, Jesus Himself tells us that we can find rest in Him. Isn't that a beautiful, gracious promise? When anxious thoughts grip our throats, we fight back by running to Christ who gives us refuge and rest. When burdens bear heavily on our shoulders, we return to Jesus Christ for reprieve. When fears are relentless, anxiety merciless, and depression too deep to bear, we run to Jesus because there's no place that offers us more safety.

We plant ourselves firmly before the Lord. We make ourselves unyielding in the face of turmoil. And we do so only by entering into His presence, quenching our thirst on the living water of His Word and submitting ourselves to Him in prayer. For however unrelenting our anxiety might be, we by the strength of Christ need to be 100 times more. These things aren't necessarily easy tasks. They take effort and gusto on our part, and above all they require us to enter into the presence of God, taking hold of His Word and implanting its power within us by the movement of the Holy Spirit.

When we take on the yoke of Christ, learning from all of His ways, our hearts and posture are transformed. We know that Jesus Christ endured everything that we endure on this earth and successfully lived a life without sin (Hebrews 2:18, 4:15). That means that He surely did experience the temptation to participate in anxiety, yet He withheld Himself from that participation. He remained sinless. In so doing, we have a perfect sympathizer in Him, as well as a perfect refuge when we're in need of strength and courage. We then must make a decision on whether or not to join ourselves together with Him by a yoke and take on His burden, which He promises is easy and light.

So, then we take on His yoke. We put on His character. We lay ourselves and our burdens down before Him, and we learn about who He is and what He's done for us. We learn to imitate His meekness and gentleness. In so doing, we are all the more strengthened and all the more equipped to flee from anxious, depressive, fearful, doubtful, difficult thoughts and emotions, and we instead seek refuge in Him.

When fears are relentless, anxiety merciless, and depression too deep to bear, we run to Jesus because there's no place that offers us more safety.

1. What are some practical ways to take on the yoke of Christ and exchange your own burdens for His?

_____

2. Read Hebrews 2:18 and 4:15. How do these verses grow your understanding of Christ as our perfect sympathizer?

_____

3. How does imitating Jesus Christ give us help in fleeing from anxiety?

_____

COME TO ME, ALL OF YOU
WHO ARE WEARY AND
BURDENED, AND I WILL
GIVE YOU REST.

Matthew 11:28

weekly reflection

What are some of the prominent things you've learned this week?

What are some practical ways to implement what you've learned this week in your daily life?

What did this week's reading teach you about the state of mankind/sin?

Pick a verse/passage from this week's reading and paraphrase it in your own words.

This week, implement the practice of thinking upon the character of God and our hope in heaven every time anxiety seizes you. In what ways can this train your brain to be more consumed with God than with the things of this world?

What are some goals/desires you have for growing in your relationship with God this week? List them below.

week two

—

DAY ONE

2 Corinthians 10:3-5

For although we live in the flesh, we do not wage war according to the flesh, since the weapons of
our warfare are not of the flesh but are powerful through God for the demolition of strongholds.
We demolish arguments and every proud thing that is raised up against the knowledge of God,
and we take every thought captive to obey Christ.

We live in a Genesis 3 world and wage war against it every day that we're in it. There's no escaping the effects of the fall. One very real, very tangible effect of the fall in our everyday life is our propensity to be consumed with worrying, doubting that God is who He says He is. But feelings aren't facts, and anxiety is often a cunning liar. Because the battle we're in is spiritual rather than physical, 2 Corinthians 10:3-5 gives us some insight into this war and the weapons we have in our arsenal that benefit our waging. We don't fight against flesh; our wounds are not in our skin. We fight against unseen principalities and our scars are mental and spiritual.

We don't fight with sharp steel blades, but what we do use to fight with is far more powerful and yields a much deadlier blow to the enemy. Our weapons are powered by God and are purposed by Him to defeat and demolish the strongholds of Satan. God's weaponry can defeat the lies that Satan whispers in our ears. The sword forged by the Spirit is undefeated.

This passage from 2 Corinthians tells us that we are enabled to demolish the strongholds of sin and evil in our lives—that includes, but is not limited to, anxiety, depression, and fear that we experience. By the power of God, we demolish anxiety, we flee from the enticement of sin, and we are exalted in the knowledge of Jesus Christ. We pull apart, piece by piece, every faulty argument that the devil gives us because of the power of having the knowledge of God.

Did you catch that? That's what the weapon is—knowledge. But not merely knowledge, not simply facts. *Divine knowledge.* Knowledge that comes from above. Knowledge that shapes us inwardly and outwardly. Knowledge that empowers us and upholds us. Knowledge that we attain from God Himself. God offers us the gracious, merciful gift of partaking in His knowledge. His knowledge will not fail, nor will it disintegrate under pressure, nor will it be weakened from age to age. His knowledge is infinite and eternal, and we are offered a stake in it.

The knowledge of God wins. It wins against any argument, any lie, any semblance of pride. We use knowledge as a weapon when we make other erroneous thoughts bow down to it. When anxiety creeps in, we extinguish it with the knowledge that Christ is alive, and our hope is in heaven. When depression overwhelms us, we destroy it with the understanding that the sacrifice of Christ is sufficient for our everlasting joy. When doubt and fear constrict us, we mute it with the wisdom that God is far more able to complete the daunting tasks before us. We take the unwanted thoughts captive and we force them into subjection of Christ Himself, making them obey Him.

When anxiety tempts us, we must recognize it as such. In identifying it in this way, we are more able to take the thoughts captive and put them before the throne of God for Him to abolish. We smother these unwanted thoughts by reminding ourselves of who God is, what He has done, and the remarkable power and authority He has over sin, death, and Hades. When we dwell on His sufficiency, when we think on His holy purity, when we consider His ultimate authority, the troubles of this world begin to dim. When we cause ourselves to think with an eternal perspective as we ought to, we are empowered by the Spirit to draw our eyes upward, away from the wretched things of this world and toward the glorious riches of God Almighty.

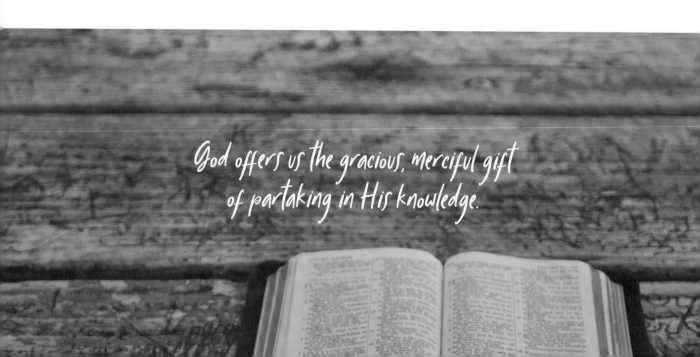

God offers us the gracious, merciful gift of partaking in His knowledge.

1. How does thinking on the character of God offer you hope in your daily life?

_____

2. What are some practical ways to take captive your thoughts and make them obey Jesus Christ?

_____

3. In what ways is God far more sufficient to handle our intrusive thoughts than we are?

_____

week two

—

DAY TWO

1 Peter 5:6-7

Humble yourselves, therefore, under the mighty hand of God, so that he may exalt you at the proper time, casting all your cares on him, because he cares about you.

In this book, Peter is speaking to a group of exiles displaced in the atrocities and horrors of Nero's rule. These are people who've been ripped from their homes and families and thrust into a foreign land among people who do not share the same faith in Jesus Christ that they do. They were likely lonely. They were likely frustrated and angry. And apparently, they were prone to anxious thoughts. Peter takes the opportunity to exhort these displaced Christians through this letter, reminding them of the eternal inheritance they have in Christ, encouraging them to remain faithful and holy in the midst of a new context.

Now the apostle is taking a moment, albeit brief, to speak to them about anxiety. Peter gives us two things to think and act upon in this passage. He first tells of the value of humility, and second, he tells of the value of casting our cares upon God. These two things go hand-in-hand because submitting and humbling ourselves under God's hand is essential to our ability to successfully cast our anxieties on Him. We will find ourselves unable to cast our worries into God's sovereign hand if we refuse to recognize His hand as sovereign and ours as not. We can only give anxiety over to God when we humble ourselves before Him, recognizing that He is God and we are not, knowing that He is far more capable of working in and through the good and bad things in our lives.

It is important to talk about humility during the discussion of anxiety. Humility is necessary in our relationship with God. Recognizing that God is all-powerful, all-knowing, and in complete control delivers harmony to the conversation of worry and doubt. Seeing and believing that God is the divine orchestrator grows us in our faith. Submitting to God through the knowledge that He sees everything and we do not is imperative to loosening the grip that we have on the things of this world. The exiles that Peter wrote to were ripped from their homes and thrust into a foreign land. Humbling themselves before God looked like acknowledging that though their circumstances would be deemed worthy by the world of anxious worry, that there was no need to worry at all. God had a plan to grow them, sanctify them, and exalt them.

Peter doesn't just demand that Christians behave a certain way or commit certain acts and not tell us why we should do so. Why should we humble ourselves under His powerful hand? Because God wants to exalt us at the proper time when all things are made new and we enjoy our eternal inheritance along with Christ. Why should we give our burden of anxiety to God? Because He cares for us. We humble ourselves because He wants to exalt us, and we give Him our burdens because He cares that we're comforted. God doesn't ask for our humility and our letting go of anxiety baselessly. He asks for this from us because He wants something better for us. In exchange for pride, He will exalt us. In exchange for the participation in anxiety, He will care for us. That's a glorious exchange.

Why should we give our burden of anxiety to God?
Because He cares for us.

1. What are some practical ways that you can humble yourself before the Lord?

2. What are some of the most difficult aspects of trusting God and humbling yourself before Him?

3. How does the fact that God cares for you impact your ability to humble yourself and cast your cares upon Him?

week
two

DAY THREE

Matthew 6:25-34

Therefore I tell you: Don't worry about your life, what you will eat or what you will drink; or about your body, what you will wear. Isn't life more than food and the body more than clothing? Consider the birds of the sky: They don't sow or reap or gather into barns, yet your heavenly Father feeds them. Aren't you worth more than they? Can any of you add one moment to his life-span by worrying? And why do you worry about clothes? Observe how the wildflowers of the field grow: They don't labor or spin thread. Yet I tell you that not even Solomon in all his splendor was adorned like one of these. If that's how God clothes the grass of the field, which is here today and thrown into the furnace tomorrow, won't he do much more for you—you of little faith? So don't worry, saying, 'What will we eat?' or 'What will we drink?' or 'What will we wear?' For the Gentiles eagerly seek all these things, and your heavenly Father knows that you need them. But seek first the kingdom of God and his righteousness, and all these things will be provided for you. Therefore don't worry about tomorrow, because tomorrow will worry about itself. Each day has enough trouble of its own.

This passage begins with a key word: *therefore.* "Therefore" means that the proceeding words have a direct correlation with the preceding ones. In order to grasp more fully what Jesus' words and commands are in this passage, we've got to be aware of what he was just saying before this. In verses 19-24, Jesus teaches something extraordinary: this world is not where our treasure is found. He implores His people to store up treasures in heaven instead of on earth, telling of the unbreakable security that heaven offers, while also reminding us that we can't actually serve two masters.

Jesus is urging His people to remember that precious metals tarnish, money loses its value, and that earthly things will inevitably rot away. This seems like just cause for worry, doesn't it? Jesus is telling us that the things of earth, the things that we can physically and tangibly touch and feel, will one day be no more. We can't rely on them. Moths will chew them up, and rust with dissolve it all. It can be a frightening thing to think about the brevity of this life, knowing that all that is surrounding us in any given moment will pass away. As believers in Christ, God is imploring us to remember this everyday and live accordingly, having eternal things impressed upon our hearts and minds. Looking to the future in this way can be frightening; exercising our faith with total and utter reliance on our future inheritance in heaven can be daunting.

Perhaps this is part of the reason why Christ then launches into a lesson about anxiety and worry. Because we store up hope and security in eternal things, we need not worry about clothes. Because of the riches awaiting us in heaven, we need not worry about fine clothing. Because we look forward to forever communion with God, we are able to recognize the temporary things of this world for what they are—vanishing. Not only does Christ's call to store up eternal treasures remind us of the futility of placing our hope in this world, but it emphasizes the true things that will matter forever. The things that will outlast our corporeal bodies and this corporeal world are the things worth our time and energy. As believers, we are tasked with not being consumed with worry about the present things of the world—what we will eat, drink, or wear. Instead, we are consumed with Christ who we will enjoy in everlasting life.

Finally, this passage is a call to remember the things that God tends to with unrelenting attention. Jesus isn't telling us not to worry about food because we do not need it, nor drink because we survive without it, nor clothing because nakedness isn't vulnerable. He is telling us not to worry because our Father in heaven is in complete, sovereign control of these circumstances. Christ calls to our minds the splendor of the lilies—do they do anything on their own part to exude such beauty? No, it is only by the Father's will. He draws our attention to the birds—have they farmed a day in their life, reaping and sowing? No, it is only by the Father's hand that they are fed. Birds and lilies do not have the Imago Dei, yet God tenderly cares for them, never forgetting or neglecting to feed or dress them in abundance.

What we see in this passage is a confirmation of what we read in 1 Peter. God cares for us. Jesus is encouraging believers not to simply forsake worrying, but to do so with the understanding that God cares for His people. God see us. God knows us. God loves us. He is benevolent and tender toward the lilies of the field and the birds of the sky, and if He is such to them, how much more so is He toward us who bear His image? We can trust God to know our circumstances, anticipating the things that we need, both for survival and for pleasure. Jesus continues on saying, "But seek first the kingdom of God and His righteousness, and all these things will be provided for you." Let us seek God's kingdom before our own. Let us pine after Him, His gospel, and His purpose, knowing that He will certainly be attentive to our needs when we are wholly focused on Him.

1. What are some additional things that God takes care of without fail? How can these things be a comfort to you?

_____

2. In what ways do you see 1 Peter 5:6-7 exemplified in this passage?

_____

3. What are some practical ways that we can seek God's kingdom? How can this help us flee from anxious thoughts?

_____

week two

DAY FOUR

Psalm 34:17-18

The righteous cry out, and the Lord hears, and rescues them from all their troubles.
The Lord is near the brokenhearted; he saves those crushed in spirit.

Within the pages of our Bibles we have the revelation of who God is. He has so graciously gifted us with His Word, penned by the Holy Spirit through man, so that we can know Him and have a relationship with Him. This is God's great love for us. This grand redemption that all believers experience is intrinsic to who God is. He is loving, merciful, just, kind, all-knowing, all-present, and everywhere all at once. This passage from Psalm 34 is a great reminder of the Lord's goodness and tenderness toward His people. He hears us. He hears our cries and pleas. He doesn't leave us, forsaking or abandoning us amid dire trauma. Instead, He rescues us from trouble and harm. He is close to those with broken hearts and protects those who have been crushed by life's harmful blows. Though this sometimes doesn't feel true, we can rest in blessed assurance that it is. How can we *know* that this is true? Because it is the entire story of the Bible.

From Genesis to Revelation, we have one big, overarching, redemptive story about God's great and unfathomable love for us. In Genesis 3:15, we see that though mankind fell and was cursed through sin, God promised a Savior that would mend the brokenness of it all. We see through the provision of the law that God wanted to dwell with His people so much that He provided laws of sacrifice, purity, and priesthood—all of which enabled Him to dwell with His people and His people to dwell with Him in holiness. In the prophets, we see God promise over and over that there will be a Righteous King born into the world, who would bear the weight of humanity's sin and become the sacrifice for us all. In the Gospels, we see the miracle of that Righteous King's birth, born of a virgin in humble means, the divine Son of God put to death on the cross, but reigning victorious over sin and death in His glorious resurrection. And in Revelation, we see the hope that is to come—that Righteous King will return for His people, making all things new.

Do you trust God with your eternal soul? Do you trust that He has sent Jesus Christ to redeem you? Do you believe that there will be a day when all things are made new and when God personally wipes away every tear from your eyes? We *can* trust and believe these precepts. Scripture proclaims this over and over again. If we can trust God with the eternal, can we not trust Him with the temporal?

We have more than enough reason to trust our heavenly Father and give over to Him our anxiety, worry, fear, and doubt. He has already proven His love for us time and time again. We have to diligently commit to continually preaching the gospel to ourselves. *In season and out of season.* When you feel desperate, preach the gospel to yourself. When you feel joyful, preach the gospel to yourself. At whatever cost to your pride or earthly comfort, preach the gospel to yourself and remember the character of God. He is near, and He has promised us rescue.

We have to diligently commit to continually preaching the gospel to ourselves. In season and out of season.

1. How does the redemptive story of God's love from Genesis to Revelation help grow your confidence and trust in the Lord?

_____

2. What aspects of God's character do you see in Psalm 34:18?

_____

3. What do you think it looks like for God to be near to the brokenhearted and save the crushed in spirit? Why do you think this is important to identify?

_____

week two

—

DAY FIVE

Psalm 13

But I have trusted in your faithful love; my heart will rejoice in your deliverance
Psalm 13:5

A man after God's own heart. David was an insignificant shepherd boy from an insignificant place and an insignificant family. He would become king of God's people. He would make many, many mistakes. He would write numerous songs. He would escape certain death frequently. He would have sweet victories by the power of God, and deep, dark defeats because of the indulgence of sin. David absolutely was a man after God's own heart; his lineage would bear the Messiah to the world. But David's righteousness and love of God did not make him flawless nor did it guarantee him an easy life. David's life was filled with sorrows, sins, and enemies.

David wrote many of the psalms we have in our Bibles, and these ancient songs can be divided into five major categories: lament, praise, thanksgiving, royalty, and wisdom. As many as 67 of the 150 psalms can be categorized as lamentation. These psalms recognize the suffering of this world and provide an avenue of expression to those in the midst of plight. Songs of lament have a general pattern that they follow: pleading for deliverance, description of the problem, petition for help, and a resolution to praise and trust in God.

David begins Psalm 13 by coming to God, asking why He has forgotten His servant while simultaneously describing the depth of the problem. How long would the Lord forget David? How long will David be coerced and tormented by anxiety? This psalm begins with questions that you and I likely ask often. In verses 3-4, David moves on to a prayer, pleading with God to restore him and put his enemies to shame. The last two verses exemplify David trusting his God. Though troubles befall him, David commits to rejoice in the deliverance that he knows that God will provide. He will still praise God because of His faithful and constant generosity.

There are many things that psalms of lamentation teach us, and there are many things that this psalm in particular can show us, but one of the most prominent things that we see here is that it is okay to *feel*. David felt the distress of being chased by his enemies and running for his life. He felt anxious in his circumstances and depressed in his trials. But as surely as we see psalms of lamentation ending with trusting God, we see David recognize that his feelings aren't necessarily facts. He didn't let his feelings lie to him about the character of God. He didn't let his feelings rob him of rejoicing in all the ways that the Lord had made him victorious over the troubles of life. Our feelings can work for us or against us, and when battling the beast of anxiety, we must be diligent in identifying which category they fall into.

Feelings of anxiety, fear, or doubt can strangle us. But what if we make these harsh feelings serve us? Feelings can be used by God to draw you closer to Him. Like the psalmist, though we experience troubles of every sort on every side of our lives, we have a call placed on our lives to steward them, making sure they serve us. In our discomfort, let us learn about God and cause our minds to resound with remembrances of God's unchanging faithfulness. When sorrows roll over us, let us be faithful to God as He has been faithful to us by taking our feelings captive and making them obey Jesus Christ, causing us to remember God's goodness as we always ought to.

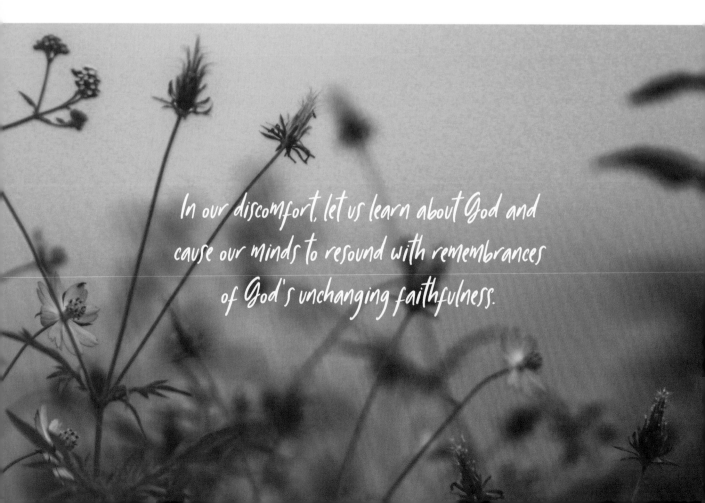

In our discomfort, let us learn about God and cause our minds to resound with remembrances of God's unchanging faithfulness.

1. What are some of the ways that our feelings can bring us closer to God?

2. What are some of the ways that our feelings can place a wedge between us and God?

3. How does preaching God's goodness and faithfulness to our feelings help shape and mold our relationship with God?

THE RIGHTEOUS CRY OUT,
AND THE LORD HEARS,
AND RESCUES THEM FROM
ALL THEIR TROUBLES.
THE LORD IS NEAR THE
BROKENHEARTED;
HE SAVES THOSE
CRUSHED IN SPIRIT.

Psalm 34:17-18

weekly reflection

What are some of the prominent things you've learned this week?

What are some practical ways to implement what you've learned this week in your daily life?

What did this week's reading teach you about the state of mankind/sin?

Pick a verse/passage from this week's reading and paraphrase it in your own words.

This week, implement the practice of thinking upon the character of God and our hope in heaven every time anxiety seizes you. In what ways can this train your brain to be more consumed with God than with the things of this world?

What are some goals/desires you have for growing in your relationship with God this week? List them below.

week three

—

DAY ONE

1 Kings 19:3-21

Then he said, "Go out and stand on the mountain in the Lord's presence."
1 Kings 19:11

Elijah was a prophet to Israel, proclaiming the Word of the Lord to the people in his reach, urging repentance, and seeking to turn wicked hearts toward God. As you might imagine, rebuking people for their wickedness didn't necessarily make Elijah a popular man, and by this point in the passage, Elijah has a bounty on his head. He is distressed. He is literally fleeing for his life and has been for some time now. He's loathed among the nation, and he's alone. He pleads to God, "I have had enough! Lord, take my life, for I am no better than my fathers." It's not dramatic to say that Elijah wanted to die. He wasn't being hyperbolic—he was being honest. Being hated and scorned weighed him down, and he was at the end of his proverbial rope. The Lord didn't smite him for this proclamation, nor did He punish him for feeling so distraught. He cooked a meal for Elijah. God filled his stomach and quenched his thirst. God provided for his physical need in that moment because he was about to endure a long journey.

After 40 days of travel, Elijah comes to rest upon the mountain of God and experiences the Lord in a peculiar yet powerful way. An earth-shattering wind comes through, but the Lord isn't in it. The ground shifts and shakes, but the Lord isn't in the earthquake. A fire appears, but the Lord was not in that either. The Lord wasn't found in earth-shattering circumstances, but He was found in a soft whisper. The Lord was gentle with the prophet Elijah. He was tender toward His servant and instructed Elijah to pass the baton of prophet to a man named Elisha. From 1 Kings 20 through 2 King 2, we see the relationship between Elijah and Elisha. Elisha was the prophet's protégé and student. Elijah instructed and taught Elisha, all the way until Elijah was carried up to the heavens in a chariot of fire.

First the Lord answered the distress of Elijah by simply providing him with food, but secondly (perhaps more significantly) God provided Elijah with a companion. He sent to him a man with whom he could minister with, whom he could teach, who could alleviate some of the burden that Elijah himself bore. Elisha was faithful in all of these tasks. The Lord truly did provide for Elijah, alleviating the pressures that depression had gripped upon his throat.

Elijah was deeply distressed and consumed by the gravity of life to the point of pleading for the reprieve of death. God was faithful to the prophet in those moments; He cared for him gently and tenderly. He provided Elijah with fellowship with both Himself and with Elisha. The testimony of Elijah's life is one that can lift our hearts up. The witness of Elisha's love for his teacher in 2 Kings 2 is a narrative that can and should remind us of the incredible value of Christian friendship. The Lord cares for His people and attends to them diligently and loyally, and seeing these characteristics of God played out in these chapters should grow and expand the trust we have in our Savior. When we read of God's faithfulness to other saints within the pages of the Bible, we can assume the same faithfulness will be afforded to us who are His children. When we see the great and marvelous things the Lord has done to take care of His children of ages past, we become emboldened to give our burdens over to the foot of the throne of God, knowing that He will care for us, tenderly and graciously.

When we read of God's faithfulness to other saints within the pages of the Bible, we can assume the same faithfulness will be afforded to us who are His children.

1. How does reading the testimony of Elijah and Elisha strengthen your confidence in God?

_____

2. Why is Christian friendship so important? How is the need for Christian friendship solved in the local church?

_____

3. Spend some time in reflection. What are some of the ways that God has been gentle and tender toward you in your distress? Why are these things important to recall?

_____

week three

—

DAY TWO

Hebrews 4:14-16

Therefore, since we have a great high priest who has passed through the heavens—Jesus the Son of God— let us hold fast to our confession. For we do not have a high priest who is unable to sympathize with our weaknesses, but one who has been tempted in every way as we are, yet without sin. Therefore, let us approach the throne of grace with boldness, so that we may receive mercy and find grace to help us in time of need.

We have hope before us, available for us to partake in. We have the hope and consolation that Jesus Christ sympathizes with everything we might experience this side of heaven. Temptation? He was tempted by Satan himself. Grief? He was forsaken by God the Father on the cross, bearing the highest degree of grief. Shamed? He was stripped bare before a nation before being brutalized on the cross. Lonely? His best friends couldn't remain awake to pray with Him while in the Garden of Gethsemane, moments before His betrayal in His deepest hour of distress and despair. If you've felt it, Christ has felt it too.

This isn't a one-up situation either. The author of Hebrews isn't saying, "Oh, you think you've got it bad? Look at what Jesus endured!" This isn't a competition. Instead, the author is telling us that we have a friend, a confidant, a great sympathizer in Jesus Christ. He can perfectly console us because He has felt our most desperate feelings. He can wholly comfort us because He has experienced the most brutal discomfort this world has to offer. He has felt the full weight of what this sinful earth deals to us; He has endured attacks from the enemy at every side.

We are enabled to hold fast to our confession, that is our commitment to the Lord, because of the great strength and endurance that Jesus Christ displayed and because He sympathizes with our every need. He remained sinless in this world and in His fleshly vesture. He remained sinless when tempted by fear, anxiety, and depression—even unto the point of death. Because of this we can now be bold before God; as recipients of His mercy and partakers of His grace we are able to boldly ask the Father for help regarding our every need. We ask knowing that our Savior understands our longings and fear. We ask with full faith that what we feel Jesus felt too.

When battling the invasion of anxiety on our hearts and minds we must remember the hope we have before us. This is part of what keeps us marching forward steadily and relentlessly. As believers we have the hope that Jesus Christ is a fully sufficient sympathizer for our every situation, and every day we must rely on that hope to propel us forward in sanctification. In Matthew 27:46, we read one of Jesus' last statements on the cross, "My God, My God, why have you forsaken Me?" This verse is quoting a Davidic psalm of lament, Psalm 22:1. This is a song that would have been sung by the Israelites often; undoubtedly it was a song Jesus knew well. It's a song about the deep-seated, wretched feeling of being left by our God, a song that epitomizes large swaths of the human experience. When Jesus sang this song, He was singing our song. The song that our heart cries out, "God, where are you now?" Jesus knows our song. He knows our emotions. He is our perfect sympathizer, and because of that we have abounding hope.

as recipients of His mercy and partakers of His grace we are able to boldly ask the Father for help regarding our every need.

1. What are some ways that having a sympathetic friend is helpful? How much more helpful is it to have our Savior be our sympathizer?

_____

2. Read Psalm 22. How does this help you understand Jesus' feeling on the cross?

_____

3. Spend some time in prayer, asking that God would grow your trust in Christ as your great sympathizer and grow your hope in Him during times of distress.

_____

week three

DAY THREE

Romans 8:35-39

Who can separate us from the love of Christ? Can affliction or distress or persecution or famine or nakedness or danger or sword? As it is written: Because of you we are being put to death all day long; we are counted as sheep to be slaughtered. For I am sure that neither death nor life, nor angels nor rulers, nor things present nor things to come, nor powers, nor height nor depth, nor anything else in all creation, will be able to separate us from the love of God in Christ Jesus our Lord.

The apostle Paul poses an important question here for those of us who bear a mortal struggle against anxiety. Who can separate us from God? What affliction is greater than our Heavenly Father?

It often feels like many things can separate us from the love of God. It's not uncommon for believers to be sucked into the thought that God will forsake them. It's a very real lie from hell, a very present danger to be wary of. In this passage from Romans, Paul quotes Psalm 44:22. All of Psalm 44 is a lament, pleading with God to save His people from their all-too-present adversaries, asking heartily for rescue and reprieve. Verse 22 seems to be a pivotal point in the psalm, wherein the psalmist proclaims that because of God they are experiencing affliction, even to the point of death. Don't we feel like this sometimes too? That it is because of our Christianity, because of our walk with God, because of spiritual warfare that our lives *seem* to be in shambles? For the sake of God, we experience troubles. Perhaps our struggles aren't a hinderance to our walk with God, but instead are a point of strength. Perhaps the afflictions we experience in this life, whatever they may be, are cause for us to soldier ahead by the strength of God. Perhaps the brushes we have with anxiety aren't a punishment or a fate of doom. Perhaps it is an opportunity for us to cling to the Lord, letting Him fight (and win) the battles for us.

I probably need not remind you of the close walk that Paul the apostle had with Christ. Saved by grace through faith, he was blinded by his Savior, going on to pen most of the New Testament letters that we know today. He was swept up into the third heaven. He saw unspeakably beautiful things. He gained his apostleship from the Lord, not by man, and was taught directly by the Holy Spirit. Knowing all of this makes the following verse that much more consoling: "For I am *sure*. . ." The apostle has no doubt in his mind that absolutely nothing can separate God's people from the love of God Himself. He knows it because the Lord has told him, and he knows it because he has experienced this firsthand himself. He experienced the faithfulness of God when imprisoned, when stoned, when shipwrecked, when martyred. In all of it, he intimately knew the faithfulness and steadfastness of the love of God. He knew that nothing could separate him from it.

We can rest in His love. We can retreat from anxiety in His love. We can flee depression in His love. He has dutifully carved out a cleft for each of us in His embrace, a refuge when sorrows swell and life is frightening. Psalm 44 is a lament, but the psalmist finishes the song by pleading the character of God in their dire circumstances. Psalm 44 ends with hope. Romans 8:39 leaves us with hope too. We must heed the hope that is offered to us in our Great Helper, Jesus Christ. Freedom from what ails us is available through the love of Christ, and any inkling that the love of God has left you is merely a figment.

He has dutifully carved out a cleft for each of us in His embrace, a refuge when sorrows swell and life is frightening.

1. Is there anything that you fear might separate you from the love of God? Give this over to Him in prayer, asking that He would grow your confidence in Him.

---

2. In what ways does this passage encourage you to let God fight the battles of life for you?

---

3. Read Psalm 44 as a whole. How does this expand your understanding of the passage in Romans?

week three

—

DAY FOUR

1 Corinthians 15:50-58

What I am saying, brothers and sisters, is this: Flesh and blood cannot inherit the kingdom of God, nor can corruption inherit incorruption. Listen, I am telling you a mystery: We will not all fall asleep, but we will all be changed, in a moment, in the twinkling of an eye, at the last trumpet. For the trumpet will sound, and the dead will be raised incorruptible, and we will be changed. For this corruptible body must be clothed with incorruptibility, and this mortal body must be clothed with immortality. When this corruptible body is clothed with incorruptibility, and this mortal body is clothed with immortality, then the saying that is written will take place: Death has been swallowed up in victory. Where, death, is your victory? Where, death, is your sting? The sting of death is sin, and the power of sin is the law. But thanks be to God, who gives us the victory through our Lord Jesus Christ! Therefore, my dear brothers and sisters, be steadfast, immovable, always excelling in the Lord's work, because you know that your labor in the Lord is not in vain.

Paul closes out 1 Corinthians by speaking of abounding, fruitful, bountiful hope that we have as believers. We have the hope of a final resurrection from the dead, a hope of being made whole and fully healed. A hope that is established in the realm of eternity. A hope that, like our God, is imperishable.

Our flesh, bone, and marrow are not permanent. What ails us in this life in not permanent. Our bodies are corruptible and perishable now, but they won't always be. Our skin and sinew are incapable of inheriting the kingdom of heaven, but our eternal souls are not. The anxieties that plague us, the depression that haunts us, and the fears that paralyze us—they're all corruptible, perishable, and temporal. They won't follow us into our eternal inheritance. We have a promise from God that we will be changed. We will, in an instant, be freed from the corruption of this world. We will be transformed into glorified bodies and minds. We will be perfected, made holy by Jesus Christ's righteousness and power. Then we will be incorruptible, clothed with immortality. Death will not find us, and the plagues that sin brings will follow us no more.

We have the privilege to put on such incorruptibility only by the power of Jesus Christ who defeated the grave and reigns victorious over sin and death. Death was swallowed up and defeated by Christ. While we will still taste death should the Lord's return wait, we will not experience spiritual death if we believe in Jesus Christ. Death, and all of its outpourings in our lives, has no tangible, real grip on us. The clutch of sin and death that we feel from anxiety is merely a phantom, a ghost of what once was, but now is no more. Before we were believers in Christ, perhaps the reach of death and sin from anxiety was real, but now in Jesus' name we are conquerors, defeaters of the lies Satan may throw our way. Because of Christ's victory over the grave, we share in that victory, awaiting the Day that Jesus will return for us and change us forever. Through the blood of Christ we now participate in the victory that Christ won and the gift of salvation.

Because of this, we must be steadfast, immovable, and excelling in what God asks of us. We are able to do this only by the strength of God. We share and participate in His power and strength. We become empowered to partake in the strength of God when we are being sanctified in our relationship with Him through His Word, and through His Word we are reminded of the hope we have ahead of us: total and complete healing and freedom in Christ. Because we know that Christ is not done with the world, we have hope. Because we know He's got a better place being built for us, we have hope. Because we know that sin, death, anxiety, doubt, fear, and depression can't follow us into our imperishable home, we rest assured in the grace of Jesus Christ.

Through the blood of Christ we now participate in the victory that Christ won and the gift of salvation.

1. In what ways does this passage help you shift your thinking from earthly things to heavenly things?

_____

2. Why does thinking on heavenly, eternal things enrich our walks with God?

_____

3. Spend some time in self-examination. Does the fact that the things of this world are perishing frighten or comfort you? Spend some time in prayer, asking that the Holy Spirit would help guide your thinking of eternal things.

_____

week three

—

DAY FIVE

Revelation 21:1-6

Then I saw a new heaven and a new earth; for the first heaven and the first earth had passed away, and the sea was no more. I also saw the holy city, the new Jerusalem, coming down out of heaven from God, prepared like a bride adorned for her husband. Then I heard a loud voice from the throne: Look, God's dwelling is with humanity, and he will live with them. They will be his peoples, and God himself will be with them and will be their God. He will wipe away every tear from their eyes. Death will be no more; grief, crying, and pain will be no more, because the previous things have passed away. Then the one seated on the throne said, "Look, I am making everything new." He also said, "Write, because these words are faithful and true." Then he said to me, "It is done! I am the Alpha and the Omega, the beginning and the end. I will freely give to the thirsty from the spring of the water of life.

The apostle John was gifted by Christ with this vision of what would come. John was exiled on the island of Patmos, all of his friends had died, and Jesus Christ comes to him in a vision, telling him of many great and wondrous things. This particular vision in Revelation 21 comes near the end of John's letter, and in this passage, we are allowed to marvel at the beauty, grace, and kindness of our Lord Jesus Christ.

There are five major promises that we see in these six verses. The first promise that we read is that this world isn't permanent; it will pass away and something new will come. We see this promise repeated two additional times in this passage, and many more times do we see it throughout the rest of Scripture (Isaiah 65:17-25, Matthew 24:35, 1 Corinthians 13:10, 2 Peter 3:10).

The second promise is that evil will not be allowed into what is made new. We see throughout the letter that things of the sea often represent evil, wickedness, or other antichrist-like things (Revelation 13:1, 18:21, 20:13). In the newness that is to come, there is no sea. Yes, the physical things of this world will pass away like lands and oceans, but also all wickedness will be thwarted. The sea passes away forever, symbolically marking that evil cannot and will not exist in the newness that Jesus promises and plans to bring about.

The third promise that we see in this passage is that God will once again dwell among His people. The Lord dwelt freely with Adam and Eve in the Garden of Eden until the fall happened. When sin entered the world, God's holiness couldn't live among the wickedness. He couldn't dwell with His children. In Leviticus, we see Him make a way for sinful people to live in His presence by designating rituals, priests, and purity laws. When Jesus Christ came as 100 percent man and 100 percent God, when He fulfilled every letter of the law, when He died, resurrected, and then ascended on high, He made a way for the Holy Spirit to live within us. As believers, though we have the Spirit, there still is not a perfected, finished, fullness of dwelling with God, but when what is old passes away, He will live with us and we will live with Him. He will *tabernacle* with us. This image and language of God dwelling with His people recalls back to the Old Testament tabernacle, in which the Lord dwelt in a tent in the center of His people with a pillar of cloud resting upon the tent by day and a pillar of fire resting upon it by night. We look forward to the day in which we dwell with God, fully and securely.

The fourth promise is that He will personally wipe out our grief. Not only will no evil enter into this new place, but the effects of evil, that is sin and death and every single thing that grieves us, will be no more. He will personally wipe away the tears this life has caused. We will be His people, He will be our God. Pause and reflect on the gravity of that. While we were still sinners, Christ still died for us, and while we are still imperfect, the Lord *still* wants us. We are His possession. He is our inheritance. Our God is a personal God; the Almighty wants to commune with us perfectly. This passage from Revelation encourages us that His plan in Scripture, from beginning to end, is making a way for us to commune with Him intimately.

The final promise is that He will forever give living water, quenching our thirst on His goodness forever and ever. He will fulfill our every desire and need. He will provide us with more sustenance than water. He will give us life eternal. He will freely give Himself to us, quench our thirst for joy and delight for all eternity. His words are faithful and true—we can trust that these things will come to pass. We can trust Him for our eternal happiness and freedom from anxiety. He will personally pluck-out the troubles of this life, He will personally eradicate them from the life to come, and He will dwell with us, quenching our thirst forever. There is hope to the plagues of anxiety, worry, doubt, fear, depressions, and any other things the devil hurls at us. There is hope because Jesus has a plan that is working every day to bring us to perfect communion with Him. Christian, take heart that anxiety, depression, and fear are not permanent. The old will pass away, and the new will certainly come.

1. How does meditating on this passage shape your perspective on anxiety?

2. How does this passage grow your understanding of God's character?

3. In what ways does this passage impact the way you understand the rest of Scripture?

THEREFORE, LET US
APPROACH THE THRONE
OF GRACE WITH BOLDNESS,
SO THAT WE MAY RECEIVE
MERCY AND FIND GRACE TO
HELP US IN TIME OF NEED.

Hebrews 4:16

weekly reflection

What are some of the prominent things you've learned this week?

What are some practical ways to implement what you've learned this week in your daily life?

What did this week's reading teach you about the state of mankind/sin?

WEEK THREE

Pick a verse/passage from this week's reading and paraphrase it in your own words.

_____

This week, implement the practice of thinking upon the character of God and our hope in heaven every time anxiety seizes you. In what ways can this train your brain to be more consumed with God than with the things of this world?

_____

What are some goals/desires you have for growing in your relationship with God this week? List them below.

_____

FOR STUDYING GOD'S
WORD WITH US!

CONNECT WITH US:

@THEDAILYGRACECO

@KRISTINSCHMUCKER

CONTACT US:

INFO@THEDAILYGRACECO.COM

SHARE:

#THEDAILYGRACECO

#LAMPANDLIGHT

WEBSITE:

WWW.THEDAILYGRACECO.COM
